A WITCH AMONG THE GOOSEBERRIES

Ian McDonough

Mariscat
Press 2014

ISBN 978 0 946588 73 2

Acknowledgements

'The Buried Sun' was winner of the National Galleries of
Scotland poetry competition and was first published in
The Scotsman. 'Narrative Line' was first published in *Dactyl*.
'Sky Above the Back Shore, Brora', 'Sky Above Premier Inn,
Inverness', and 'Postcards of Silloth' were first published in
the *Edinburgh Review*.

With thanks to Ruth Bailey for the drawing of the witch.

Designed and typeset by Gerry Cambridge
in Comenius Pro
gerry.cambridge@btinternet.com

Printed by Glasgow Print & Design Centre
130 Douglas Street, Glasgow G2 4HF
www.GlasgowPDC.co.uk

Published by Mariscat Press, 10 Bell Place, Edinburgh EH3 5HT
hamish.whyte@btinternet.com
www.mariscatpress.com

Contents

In memory of
Catherine McDonough and Maureen Bailey:
two audacious women
who showed us how to be alive

SIGHTINGS

A Witch Among the Gooseberries

In the garden of the house where I was born
a witch lived among the gooseberries.
I never met her
but I'm certain she was there,
her hair wild and curly,
eyes akimbo, black dress torn.

Come the school holidays,
as I lay stretched on the heat-soaked ground,
she'd whisper improprieties in my ear,
sing bawdy airs that scorched the lawn.
Later, above summer night-time gales
I'd hear her shriek
in barbarous tongues
I couldn't help but understand.

I hear her now, faint but strident,
complaining I've forgotten how to see her.
Still she stirs my tired blood,
urging me to tear off my grey shirt,
make wild my greying hair
lie down beside her in the gooseberries.

Wonders of the Solar System

1.

Monday was washing day: us kids
dragging our feet through the suds,
drawing pentacles on the kitchen floor.

In the Free Church manse, the minister's wife
has locked him in the cellar,
his cheeks crimson with lust and indignation.

The TV lounge of the Sutherland Arms Hotel
is empty: no-one is watching the expanding universe
save a solitary mouse, lost in amazement.

2.

Sporting a full-length cream mackintosh
and a wide-brimmed fedora,
the birdman of Edinburgh
walks every morning to the park
with a paper bag of breadcrumbs.

A benevolent dictator, he grants
favour to every citizen.
They flock around his feet,
fussing and scolding each other,
pecking up his gifts, uttering
deep coos of recognition and fealty.

The emperor of the pigeons
dallies for hours among his subjects,
blessed by purpose, his standing secure
under the cold, swinging stars.

3.

In the school I reluctantly attended
Mars was the presiding planetary influence.
A ruddy glow suffused our cheeks—
in the playground blood flowed
and spilled, spilled and flowed
under that martial radiance.

Nobody informed us the influence
was malign, but after a while
most of us guessed for ourselves.
Only a few stayed loyal, flailing
through their later years
in desolate tribute.

4.

We're waiting for the sun to break the clouds,
and then we'll carry costumes, towels and water
across the machair to the little beach.

Far away, emails are being exchanged,
snap decisions made and instantly regretted:
towering edifices rise and fall.

Even further, hydrogen atoms are being cracked,
feeding a furnace that scatters rays
a million miles through space to bronze our skins.

Summoning

When your heart becomes night
and the night's heart is pitch
find a quiet corner
in the noiseless room.

Leave a bowl of milk,
a trace of blood,
a little salt.

Now be still as stone.

Quick enough your shade will come.

Snare the shade in light,
bind it on an oath,
ask it when the thing
we once were promised
will arrive.

Titania

Deep in the wood I sew up leaves,
flay branches, bodge old stones,
wash linen
in a goblin's blood.

Geese honk, an owl calls *twenty-two*,
and through the trees, my love, you race
with pants on fire.

I am so silver, flint and ancient grey. My eyes
cast shadows.
If I could gift you one long golden day,
what bright Mycelia might drive
slow filaments
into your headlong noon?

I wait, recumbent, lusting in my bower,
pining for your vitamins, your calcium,
the stuff that makes
a host of titmice chirrup
in among the weary fleshless flowers.

My faeries pleasure me, leaving not a single mark.
Here, where the mornings are so dark,
you could be king of cobwebs, play a lord,
hear guitars tune themselves,
watch threads construct their loom.
All you must give me is your beating, transient heart.

Toy Farm

Flanked by wooden trees
the plastic Friesians stand and stand.
Beyond his model house
a tiny farmer
leans forever on a cross-barred gate.
I hear him utter nothing to his silent dog.

My shadow falls over the farm:
insanely, I am swept by pity
for the plastic farmer and his plastic dogs and cows
because my shadow moves across the farm.

Because I watch my shadow move across the farm.

The Buried Sun

—Rembrandt Van Ryn: Self Portrait

Aged two, they said, I drew the outline of a sparrow in the dirt.
Soon my eye consumed the whole of Leyden,
fingers etched with light, ears burning
with a score of crafty secrets from old Swanenburch,
Pieter Lastmann's recipe for clouds.

Fast enough I left them, the old devils, to their tricks,
set out to snare the glory of our world. Year on year,
rejoicing, aching, among gesso chalk and glue,
layering imprimatura till my boards yielded such glow
you'd swear the sun lay buried just beneath the floor.

Older, I turned rougher with the brush, capturing
nothing more or less than I bore witness to.
This blanket of years, sewing such a bleak embroidery,
presses heavy as time rolls, stifling the blaze to smoulders,
Ochre to Raw Umber, then the frightful edges of Bone Black.

Complexity

It is seven a.m. in the campsite. Someone
is doing yoga; a divorced father from Manchester
is frying bacon for his boys; the Austrians
are packing to leave, everything stored
in measured compartments, as though
nature required a vigorous spring clean.

Capricorn is on the cusp of the House of Venus,
a fortunate alignment for the week to come.

The camping field, like everywhere else,
is being constantly bombarded by neutrinos,
passing undetected without a glance.

A nearby Dalmatian has smelled the bacon,
is whimpering relentlessly. All round the field
campers wake, starting to apply
a hundred small but well-considered fixes
to their temporary corner of boundless space.

Station Terrace

Behind the red brick railway houses
a narrow road
skirts a narrow park,
ending at The Narrow Palace.

Inside its stone-strewn garden
a child fires arrows
at your narrow heart, piercing
acquiescent flesh, releasing
perfumes of young violets and ammonia.

Might you have passed here once before,
on that narrow voyage to your future?
Sometimes, in the narrowness of our path,
it is hard with certainty to know.

Long Chalk

Ghosts of plesiosaurs, traced
in the sediment, stretch
snaking heavy necks
up towards the future.

Leaving the museum,
I cough through the traffic,
the clean air above
far beyond my reach.

Taking refuge in The Blind Beggar,
I watch a darts match,
rapidly descending scores
chalked carefully on the board.

Choked by rules, we brief survivors
reckon everything, weigh nothing.

POEMS BY GHOSTS

A Scent of Hyacinths

Rather abruptly I found myself dead:
there was the usual afternoon lull,
disturbed briefly by the deacon's Red Setter
fleeing persecution from these darling children,
and I remember, as I rose from my chair
to take a stroll round the garden,
a scent of hyacinths in the hall,
sharp and bright, with the vaguest hint of urine.

Then star shells—a blow I suppose—and
I was, so to speak, unincorporated.
I knew at once what had happened,
but it didn't seem to require any action,
just waiting and watching ineffectually.
In death as in life, I reflected coldly.

Bad Day in the Attic

Bricked up between walls
what else can I do
but revisit your hateful behaviour?

Do not doubt. I remember
the day you ran back
to your father in his lair,
among those model railways
and his subjugated, pimply sons.

And do not doubt I remember
the February day I came for you,
to find you laughing with your brothers,
drinking vodka sours inside
the filthy richness of his summer house.

Particularly, I recall the youngest, Roderick,
how he passed a blade between my ribs,
and how they dragged me up here, lifeless,
setting to work with crowbars, trowels, and nails.

Now my voice is weak, carried
only by the wind-stirred dust.
But when the moon swells up and bursts
as did my heart,
darling I will burst my strictures too.
Then you will hear me howl and howl and howl.

Hairyback

When no-one is watching but the kids
I crawl out of the fireplace,
grimace, girn, sport,
gesticulate,
return.

Not much of a trick, you might think
but the children are impressed
and I've frequently spoiled the cat's day.

Who am I? I've forgotten. Maybe
a bad one, maybe a fool? Maybe
a victim, though I guess I'd have deserved it.

All I know—I have this urge
for scaring. Keeps me
from remembering bells
and boiling water,
bibles, manacles, a cross.
And fire…oh, the fire!

PsychoBilly

Ah'd nivvur say ah wus evur
thu full shillin', ken?
But when thu factury closed doon,
an ma maw threw me oot,
ah startit on thae wee blue pills.
Aftur a while it wus two litres o cider
fur breakfast an' aw. Good thu first month,
drinkin' wi thu team, a wee bit theivin'
tae pay fur thu pills'n booze.

Then ah got jinky wi ma pal's missus.
Thu bastird threw me aff a car park roof.
Now here's me deid as a nympho's
vibrator battery, just hingin' an hingin' aboot.
Sometimes ah'll creep up oan some daft wee gadge,
jump oot an' shout *Dinnae be like me, man.*
But ye ken thu score, it's maistly far too late.

Pea Pod

Jacko, can you feel a cold breath
brush your cheek,
as you bank up the spuds,
thin out your rows of beans?
It was a long winter, and a hard.
Yes, hard words too between us.
She was fair, you simple. Too much it seems.

Bought and brought from the village,
I was wedded, bedded,
set to work upon your stony field,
and still a summer short of seventeen.

After our silent, scanty evening meal,
I'd dance in the garden for your eyes.
You called me your ain wee pea pod.
Certain, I was green.

One day the ceards arrived with tents and dogs and viols,
I saw their daughter stand and look. And you back.
Your breath turned hot as steam.

Jacko, your blade but her command opened my throat,
and the two lives in me cried revenge,
my blood salting your crops in its hot red stream.

Now, Jacko, your pea pod is opening her mouth
to flood your field with pest and blight,
visit her with poxes, sour her cream.

The Deep Sea Gang

Starboard-hit, she dragged us quickly down,
plunging all eighteen together
into an inexhaustible dark.
The realists opened their mouths
as soon as the water passed over our heads,
others struggled every second till the end.

At first there was panic, like falling off a roof
or being suddenly and publicly incontinent,
but soon the part of you that cares
gives up, distracted
by the spooling images behind your flooded eyes.

A fall of hours to the sea's floor,
our ship tumbling in slow, spiral arcs
and us poor sailor boys inside
starting to chatter
with whatever it is we now use for chattering—
still we don't know, or know
what binds us to the wreck.

Early on, we'd talk the big things in our lives—
lovers, families, friends. When these were worn
we turned to films, pubs, games we'd attended,
restaurants, holidays. The rule seems to be
you can't describe the same thing twice.

Surprising how quick the well runs dry.
Now, someone will pronounce *Accrington* or *celery*
or *beige*. A year later, or maybe a century,
someone else will utter *butter knife*.
Maybe when there is nothing left to tell
we will be free—but who can say?

POEMS FOR GHOSTS

Jesus in the Woods

I used to think that Jesus lived
in the woods, with leaves
in his hair, his bare brown feet
padding swiftly
along secret, shaded paths.

I thought if I could sneak down
from my room
to the midnight forest
I would hear him singing psalms
as he ran through the trees
executing one miracle after another.

When I learned from my teacher
that he lived in a land
of dust and sand and stone I felt sorry
for the trees—and for Jesus too.
But mostly for myself, knowing that
from now on, my midnight
would be quieter,
so much less interesting.

Still, in the wind-blown early hours,
I sometimes hear, among
the sighing of the rowan and the birch,
quick footsteps,
a snatch of holy song.

Gulberwick, Shetland

We will build a church at Gulberwick
from the bones of saints
washed up by the sea
and raise a steeple
from a driftwood spar
on this island with no trees.

The saints will gaze out fiercely
from the ghosts of their poor eyes.
In the storm of their looking
fruit will grow from the midden,
and the angry men of the North
will be sore consumed by love.

Bones of Thule, softening
under constant gales of time,
rock of the Word, hardening
to diamond
in the mouths of righteous men,
the tenderness of stone
be with us,
the flint of prayer
be with us,
the sharpened spear of our vision
be with us always.

East Sutherland 1969

Age fourteen, swank in flared Levis,
Chelsea boots, bead chokers, tie and dye,
we formed a home-grown village tribe.

Evenings and weekends we decorated walls—
the car park of the Sutherland Arms,
the amphitheatre of the Fountain Square—
anywhere our difference might be recognised.
And as our hair grew wild and long
the local fuzz cars
chanced more frequently to idle by.

Like any small-town stars
we gazed into the distance, waiting
for the Aliens to arrive
and free us from this blinking galaxy of local lives.

They never came. Instead,
scattered by college, pregnancy,
entropy and bars,
our tribe somehow forgot its name.

Sometimes, back here on holiday,
two former small town stars collide.
We smile, trading a look like postcards
from a man who's been abroad for such a time
he's clean forgotten how to get back home.

Narrative Line

There was a train.
And in a carriage on that train
there sat a boy.

He did not know it
(how could he know it?)
but there was a break ahead
in the narrative line.

The train derailed.
It morphed into a horse
charging through fields of gold
the boy joyfully astride.
Only now the boy was a grandmother.

How she laughed
as the wind blew up her skirt,
little knowing
that her narrative path
would soon forsake the fields
for open sea.

The horse turned to a whale:
Grandmother grew whiskers
then was swallowed whole.
Inside the whale
a captain dreamed of trains.

And then the narrative self-repaired.
Inside the train a young boy dreamed of whales.

Sky Above the Back Shore, Brora

Stunned by the unexpected northern August heat
we lay on dunes like heaps of stranded laundry.
My mother, swaddled by her children, and by theirs,
still pierced by the steel blade of my father's passing,
stared without desire at the blank horizon.

Conversation dimmed: flat on our backs
we cast our eyes up to fair weather cumulus.
A radio played 'Something in the Air',
I tried to conjure up a future past this place, this time,
but drifted back, defeated by the sun, into an absence.

All of us were locked so tight inside that absence,
made more surreal and bitter by the summer radiance.
The North Sea glinted, fulmars wheeled,
beside the waterfall we listened to small finches sing,
but a door had slammed, its echo fading down an empty hall.

Sky Above Premier Travel Inn, Inverness

Some ancient Celtic water god
is emptying the contents of his stomach
over the streets of this rural city.

I'm peering upwards hopefully,
but an all-absorbing blackness
only serves to mark the vacuum in his eyes.

Have mercy on us, water god,
we who roam from Travelodge to Travel Inn,
chasing the faint smiles of strangers.

After the rain, high grey wisps pattern the dark
like flecks from the water god's foaming maw.

I slip the outside world beneath my bed.

Morning reassembles me, glues back together
all the flimsy furniture that sleep has trashed.

Postcards Of Silloth

If love is possible—and the world
is impossible without it—then it is here
among the caravans, the ornamental
rose gardens, inside Alfredo's
Rapid Pizza Palace
that we must hunt it down.

Love will pronounce itself reluctantly,
slurring after six advocaat and lemonades,
wincing and twitching
as if at any moment
you might belt it one right on the mouth
for sheer presumption. As well you might.

Love's face will open, like the over-ripe peach
it surely is. And you will notice
that love's head is bruised
and giant—moist and buzzing
like a hive of bees. Its words are indistinct
drowned out by roaring midnight juggernauts.
You lean towards it, let it lick your ear.
Then it will lisp that famous, fatuous, line—
Now that you've caught me, you can never leave.

Raging round the world, somehow you end up home,
finding your letter-box is blocked
with postcard views of Silloth—docks
where hulks are rendered down to dust,
bold seas in arms against the Cambrian rock,
the chalk-mark on that pavement
where love slipped its silver blade between your ribs.

Evening, Ardrishaig

The loch's sunset plumage
is pure ice-cream sundae.

A shop shuts its red door
then

the heavens open.

Three teenage village vampires
return hungry
to their homes.

From the crumbling public bar
one man
sings his endless love,

drowning
in a monsoon
of cider-sweetened pain.

Truffles

Tossed into my messy cross between paella and risotto,
little slivers of the earth,
filling the kitchen with aromas of chocolate, perfume,
hung meat, dust and sex.
Eating the dish, there was a sense
of new-discovered flavours,
each speaking directly to your passing life.

We sat around the table, adults and kids,
spooning up meaning, holding our days
up to the light, drinking and drinking
and drinking
the scented Tarragona night.

Is this how death approaches us? A mouthful
of new taste, a slightly different angle of approach,
an ending and beginning startlingly combined?